# THE BEAUTY OF

## INTOLERANCE

### SETTING A GENERATION FREE TO KNOW
#### —— TRUTH & LOVE ——

Study Guide for Individuals and Adult Groups

# THE BEAUTY OF

# INTOLERANCE

## SETTING A GENERATION FREE TO KNOW
## TRUTH & LOVE

Study Guide for Individuals and Adult Groups

## JOSH MCDOWELL
## SEAN MCDOWELL

**SHILOH RUN** PRESS
An Imprint of Barbour Publishing, Inc.

# CONTENTS

# ABOUT THE AUTHORS

Authors Josh McDowell and Sean McDowell collaborated with their writer to bring you this study guide. The content is based on the McDowells' book *The Beauty of Intolerance*.

Over fifty years, Josh McDowell has spoken to more than 25 million people in 128 countries about the evidence for Christianity and the difference the Christian faith makes in the world. He has authored or coauthored more than 145 books (with more than 55 million copies in print), including such classics as *More Than a Carpenter* and *New Evidence That Demands a Verdict*. Josh and his wife Dottie have been married for more than forty-five years and have four grown children and ten grandchildren. They live in Southern California.

Sean McDowell, PhD, is an assistant professor at Biola University in the MA Christian apologetics program. He is also a bestselling author of more than fifteen books. Sean is an internationally recognized speaker for conferences, universities, schools, and churches. He and his wife Stephanie and their three children live in Southern California.

# ACKNOWLEDGMENTS

We would like to thank the following people for their contribution to this study guide:

*Don Kencke* for his insights and attention to detail as he reviewed the manuscript.

*Amanda Price* for her editorial skills in bringing the manuscript to completion.

*Kelly McIntosh* and *Tim Martins* of Barbour Publishing for their vision and passion to provide the body of Christ with this study tool to more deeply experience *The Beauty of Intolerance* message.

Josh McDowell
Sean McDowell

# How to Get the Most Out of This Study

This five-session *The Beauty of Intolerance Study Guide* can be used by small groups or individually apart from a group. While you can answer the questions throughout this guide from your own knowledge and the scripture references given, you will get the most out of this experience if you read *The Beauty of Intolerance*, which is the companion book to this study. You will be assigned chapter readings at the end of each session.

If you have not already obtained a copy of the book, you can purchase one at your local Christian supplier, order directly from the publisher by calling 1-800-852-8010, or order online at www.barbourbooks.com.

The purpose of this study is to help you and your family counter the influence of cultural tolerance. It is designed to help provide clarity on today's cultural view of tolerance, detect its inaccuracies, and offer practical insight on the following:

- Who created moral truth and its purpose
- How to live out a biblical view of tolerance with people with whom you disagree
- How to lead your family to understand God's gift of sexual morality and the universality of moral truth, and how to express love and acceptance not based on performance

Our hope is that you will become better equipped to raise up a generation to embrace a value system based on God and his Word so they can live as "'children of God without fault in a warped and crooked generation.' Then [they] will shine among them like stars in the sky" (Philippians 2:15 NIV).

# WHAT DOES IT MEAN TO BE TOLERANT?

## WHAT DO YOU THINK?

None of us is perfectly perfect. We all have sinned and are in need of forgiveness. Even in the best of relationships with others, we make mistakes, outright blow it, and need people to be patient, understanding, and tolerant of us.

What is your earliest memory of someone (a parent, teacher, friend, etc.) who demonstrated an understanding heart and tolerated your misbehavior with patience and love?

_____

_____

_____

"I remember when I was \_\_(age?)\_\_ years old, I _____(did what?) _____ and _____(name) _____ responded _____(how?) _____."

Share your story.

_____

_____

_____

_____

_____

_____

_____

_____

# SESSION OBJECTIVE

**To examine how the concept of traditional tolerance has changed and how it may be affecting you and your family.**

## HOW DO YOU RESPOND?

Read Colossians 3:12–13 and 1 Corinthians 13:4–7 aloud.


Based on these verses and your general knowledge, what does it mean to be tolerant of another person? You can also include what tolerance doesn't mean.

_____

_____

_____


Have you recognized and respected other people's beliefs without sharing them?

_____

_____

_____


Have you accommodated or put up with another person's behavior in spite of his or her unacceptable actions?

_____

_____

_____

Have you ever loved a person without loving how he or she acted?

_____

_____

_____

If you were able to answer yes to some or all of those questions, you have expressed traditional tolerance. But is that the kind of tolerance our culture today is seeking? Perhaps some friends or those in your own family are seeking something more than traditional tolerance can give.

The following represents a family tension that is recurring in many homes today. A second-year college student (Renee) wants her boyfriend (Tony) to visit her at home over Christmas break. But instead of Renee and her boyfriend staying in separate rooms, she wants her mom (Teri) and dad (Kenton) to agree to them sleeping together.

Have someone in the group read the conversation aloud as it picks up with the mother responding to the idea of having Renee's boyfriend Tony as a houseguest. This is drawn from chapter 1 of *The Beauty of Intolerance*.

> "That's a wonderful idea, honey," Teri said. "Your dad and I would love it. Just let us know ahead of time which days you'll be here, and I'll have the guest room ready."
>
> Renee hesitated. "Sure, Mom. But—" She took a deep breath. "Well, like, is the guest room really necessary? I was thinking we could just stay in my room together."
>
> Teri's eyes went wide with shock, but Kenton responded first. "Don't be silly. You can't do that. You know it's not right."
>
> "I thought you'd say that," Renee responded. "I explained to Tony how you and Mom feel about that sort of thing, but

I promised to talk to you about it anyway. I don't see why you can't just accept my lifestyle choices and me. But don't worry. We'll respect your feelings and sleep in separate rooms while we're here."

Teri's heart pounded like drums. "While you're here?" Her voice went high and shrill. "What do you mean, 'while you're here'? Are you trying to tell us that you two intend to sleep together when you're not here?"

"We already do, Mom. We're in love. You don't really expect us to—"

Kenton interrupted. "I expect you to honor the morals and values your mother and I taught you all your life."

"I do," Renee countered. "That's why I agreed that we would sleep in separate rooms while we're here. But at Tony's house or at school, it's different."

Kenton tried to keep his composure. "Are you trying to tell me that Tony's parents have no problem with your sleeping together at their house?"

"No, Dad, they don't. After all, not everyone shares your views on that sort of thing, you know."

Kenton shook his head. "I know that," he said, trying to rein in his emotions. "But I certainly thought our daughter shared them."

Renee took a deep breath and spoke in a softer tone. "Dad, in many ways I do share your views. You and Mom have taught me a lot. But there are some things I have to decide for myself. What you guys decided to do before you got married was your choice. I've made my choice, and I wish you guys could respect that and not judge me. In fact, I wish you could see that these choices are just as right for me as yours were for you."

Kenton shook his head slowly. Teri stifled a sob. "I love you, honey," she said. "I just don't see how you can so easily abandon the values we raised you with."

Consider this: Renee's parents want her to do what's right. But as far as Renee is concerned, she *is* doing what's right. She feels judged because her parents seem to be holding her to their standard of sexual morality, but she doesn't embrace that same standard.

Since Renee believes it's okay to sleep with her boyfriend, should her parents consider it right for her too, and endorse her choice? And if they don't, are they being intolerant? Discuss together.

_____

_____

_____

Do you sense that young people today, and the culture at large, view the concept of tolerance differently than you do? If so, what do you think that difference is exactly?

_____

_____

_____

Have someone in the group read the following paragraphs aloud, which were adapted from chapters 1 and 2 of *The Beauty of Intolerance*.

> Two very different understandings of tolerance are at odds here. Renee, and most of her generation, in effect says, "Be tolerant of me—which includes accepting my views and acknowledging that my behavior is right for me." Many Christian adults respond with, "I'll be glad to be tolerant by accepting you and giving you the freedom to live your own life, but don't ask me to approve of your behavior or

consider it to be right." These are two differing views on tolerance.

Today when you hear the word tolerance used, it rarely has the traditional meaning of the word. In our culture, tolerance goes beyond acknowledging and respecting the differing beliefs and practices of others. This new tolerance, what we will call cultural tolerance, propagates the notion that there is no hierarchy of moral truth—all truth is equal. In traditional tolerance you grant another the right to believe and behave differently without agreeing that he or she is right. Not so with cultural tolerance. What has shifted is the equality of beliefs, values, and truth claims. In other words, not only do all people have a right to believe what they want, but no one's beliefs, values, or truth claims are any more valid than another person's. Essentially, cultural tolerance means all truth is subjective, and thus no individual truth claim should be judged or condemned as wrong.

Cultural tolerance says that what every individual believes or says is equally right and equally valid, and that no individual's beliefs or behavior should be judged or criticized. That means they believe there is no morality that is right for everyone. With that doctrine, not only do all people have an equal right to their beliefs, but they also have a right to be treated as if their beliefs as well as the beliefs of all others are equal. All values are equal. All lifestyles are equal. All truth claims are equal. Violate that tenet of cultural tolerance and you will be labeled judgmental, intolerant, and even a bigot.

Have you, or someone you know, ever been accused of being judgmental, intolerant, or even bigoted for voicing your Christian beliefs or stating what you think is morally right? Share your experience.

_____

_____

_____

In today's world, is it possible to hold to a biblically based morality, share those convictions with others, and not be labeled intolerant? Can we convey a genuine sense of acceptance of others while not approving or endorsing their behavior without them feeling rejected?

_____

_____

_____

Take the case of Todd, his son Chad, and Chad's friend Mike. Chad wants to go with Mike to the GG9 track meet that is being hosted in the city. The GG9 is the international Gay Games, and the boys want to go to watch Mike's brother race.

Have someone in the group read the following conversation aloud. Todd is responding to his son's request to go to the games.

> "Ohhhhh, those games. Yeah, I've read some about them, and uh, I'm not really comfortable with you going, son." Todd looked straight at Chad.
> "Okay, you're not comfortable, so I'm not asking you to go," Chad retorted. "But I'm comfortable going, and we've made big plans to take in the relay race. It doesn't cost anything to get in."

"Well, I'm sorry you've made plans. I'm just saying my son is not going to any gay games, and that's that," Todd stated emphatically.

"Why not?" Chad shot back. "What's the big deal?"

"Look," Todd began, leaning forward in his chair, "I don't have anything against those people personally. I just don't like them pushing their lifestyle on the rest of society with games just for them and all their gay rights agenda and everything."

"Stop it, Dad!"

"I know you boys don't like to hear this," Todd continued. "But there comes a time to stand up for what's right and decent. Homosexuality is wrong, and we shouldn't be celebrating it, for crying out loud!"

"I'm out of here," Mike said as he turned to Chad. "Text me when you get a chance." As Mike made his way out the door, Chad turned toward his father.

"I can't believe you," Chad said, his dark gaze bewildered and accusing.

"Hey, I'm just trying to help you take a stand here, Chad."

"Take a stand against my friends?"

"What are you talking about?"

"For one thing, Mike's brother is gay. His dad kicked him out of the house, and it's like you just kicked Mike out."

"Just slow down a minute here," Todd replied, raising his hand in protest. "First off, I didn't kick anyone out of our house. And second, I didn't even know Mike's brother was gay."

"It doesn't matter, Dad. The way you're against gays is just so judgmental. If I do something that you really disagree with, are you going to kick me out of the house like Mike's father did? What if I said I was gay? You would probably disown me or something, wouldn't you?"

"Okay, settle down, Chad," Todd responded.

"No, I'm not going to settle down," Chad said defiantly. "Come on, admit that you hate gays. And if I was gay, you'd hate me too, right?"

"That's ridiculous, Chad."

"It's not ridiculous!" Chad said as he turned toward the door. "I just can't believe you are full of such hate toward people who are different from you."

And with that Chad stalked out of the house, slamming the door behind him.

---

Chad's father was trying to express his belief that homosexual behavior was wrong and didn't need to be celebrated, while at the same time not rejecting homosexuals as people. Yet Chad clearly felt his dad was rejecting the gay community. There is a difference between acceptance and approval, but most of us, like Todd, struggle to know how to make a person feel accepted when we clearly disapprove of his or her behavior. Have you experienced that struggle? Or perhaps you have been on the other end of a situation when someone disapproved of you and you equally didn't feel accepted. Share your story.

_____

_____

_____

_____

Over the next four sessions we will explore, with scripture as our guide and Christ as our example, how we can genuinely accept others in Christlike love while not necessarily approving of their behavior. We will discover how real love unlocks the secret of acceptance based on the value of the person rather than on a standard of performance.

## APPLYING IT THIS WEEK

This week, share with a friend or a family member about the difference between traditional tolerance and cultural tolerance. Here are some conversation starters to help you.

1. I've been studying lately about the idea of tolerance. What does being tolerant mean to you?

_____

_____

_____

2. Our small group has been discussing the idea of being tolerant. I've been learning. . .

_____

_____

_____

3.  In a devotional time before God, read Ephesians 6:10–17. Write a prayer asking God to equip and protect you and your family in the spiritual battle in which we are all engaged.

_____

_____

_____

This week, before the next group meeting, read chapters 1 and 2 in *The Beauty of Intolerance*. Pay particular attention to why intolerance is sometimes beautiful. If you do not already have *The Beauty of Intolerance*, see page 11 or 90 for ordering information.

## CLOSE IN PRAYER

Pray that the truth you have encountered will become more real, alive, and active in your life. Use this prayer time to express your desire to more effectively love and accept others as Christ has loved and accepted you.

# THE LOSS OF MORALITY

# WHAT DO YOU THINK?

Christianity is the religion of those who, in part, believe Jesus Christ is the Son of God and that the Bible is God's inspired revelation to humanity. Reports of Global Religious Landscape indicate, however, that a little less than a third (32 percent) of the world's population is Christian; 23 percent are Muslim, 15 percent Hindu, 7 percent Buddhist, 0.2 percent Jewish, and just under 7 percent practice various folk or traditional religions, including African traditional religions, Chinese folk religions, Native American religions, as well as religions such as the Baha´i faith, Jainism, Sikhism, Taoism, Wicca, etc. Roughly 16 percent have no religious affiliation at all.*

So with the majority of the world's population believing in something other than Christianity, how comfortable are you in saying that Jesus Christ is the only way to God?

_____

_____

_____

There are many truths that people follow other than what is written in the Bible. Why should the moral truth you believe in be the only true and right moral truth? Doesn't that sound a bit intolerant? Discuss together.

_____

_____

_____

_____

*"The Global Religious Landscape," Religion & Public Life Project, Pew Research Center, Washington, DC, December 18, 2012, http://www.pewforum.org/2012/18/global-religious-landscape-exec/.

## SESSION OBJECTIVE

**To discover how the moral truth found in
the Bible is universal and why it is right
for all people in every culture for all times.**

## HOW DO YOU RESPOND?

Renee and Chad, in our last session, chafed under the idea that
someone established a morality that applies to everyone. They were
more comfortable with the idea that each person has the right
to create his or her moral code. To say that a certain morality is
universal and right for everyone seemed narrow-minded to them.

What defines moral truth? What would make a moral truth like
"Stealing is wrong" true for everyone?

_____

_____

_____

_____

Have someone in the group read the following paragraph aloud.

> Webster defines truth, in part, as "fidelity to an original
> or standard." How do you know that the study guide
> you have in your hand is actually 5½ by 8½ inches? The
> answer is that if you measure your book against a standard
> of measurement—a measuring tape—that conforms to a
> universal standard established by the International Bureau
> of Weights and Measures, you have a correct measurement.

In other words, when your 5½-by-8½-inch study guide matches the marks on the measuring tape, which in turn conforms to the original universal standard of measurement, you can definitively state your study guide is, in fact, 5½ by 8½ inches. Truth conforms precisely to the original or standard.

What would you say is the original or standard for all universal moral truth?

_____

_____

Continue reading aloud the paragraphs adapted from chapter 3 of *The Beauty of Intolerance*.

Moral truth isn't simply an abstract concept; it originates in a person who is the original and standard for morality. Jesus said, "I am the way, the truth and the life" (John 14:6). In other words, moral claims are true if they correspond to the character of God—who is the objective source for morality. God is the source of all moral truth. "He is the Rock," Moses said, "his work is perfect. . . a God of truth and without iniquity, just and right is he" (Deuteronomy 32:4 KJV). It is God's nature and character that actually determine moral truth. He defines what is right and wrong, good and evil. But truth is not first and foremost something he decides; it is something he is.

The basis of everything we call moral, the Source of every good thing, is the eternal God who is outside us, above us, and beyond us. The apostle James wrote, "Every good and perfect gift is from above, coming down from the Father of the heavenly lights, who does not change like shifting shadows" (James 1:17 NIV).

How would Renee or Chad respond if they knew that morality wasn't something they created by their own choice? What if they understood that morality was already in existence in a person who loved and accepted everyone for who he or she is? That would reframe the entire conversation between these young people and their parents. Our young people need to understand that the reason we have this concept that some things are morally right and others are wrong is not because a church propagates it or even that it is written in a book called the Bible. The moral authority of the Bible isn't found in its commands and rules. The authority of scripture is derived directly from and founded in the very character and nature of God and represented in the flesh through Jesus Christ. All moral truth resides in and comes from God.

The reason we think that there are such concepts as "fair" and "unfair" is because our Maker is a just God.

The reason love is a virtue and hatred a vice is because the God of relationships who formed us is a God of love.

The reason honesty is right and deceit is wrong is because God is true.

The reason fidelity in marriage is honorable and infidelity is not is because God is faithful.

The reason chastity is moral and promiscuity is immoral is because God is pure.

Everything that is moral, right, holy, good, and beautiful comes from the core nature of God. He doesn't choose to do holy and right things as if he is doing an experiment to see what that's like. He does holy and right things because that is who he is—his actions come out of his core nature (Genesis 18:25).

This reframes the entire discussion as to why anything is morally right or wrong. Previous to this session, how would you have answered a child who asked, "Why is stealing wrong?" Before I would have said. . .

_____

_____

_____

Many Christians say, "Stealing is wrong because the Bible says it's wrong." Others might say, "Stealing is wrong because it's unfair to others, and it hurts people when we steal from them." While that is all true, it is not the primary reason stealing is wrong and honesty is right.

How would you now explain to a child why stealing is wrong?

_____

_____

_____

Have someone in the group read the following aloud.

> We err when we see biblical rules and commands as isolated, separate from God. God gave Moses pages and pages of highly specific rules to govern the relationships and morality of his people. Each of those rules, which we call *precepts*, applies to a specific situation. But each is important because it is grounded in a *principle*, which is a fundamental, primary law from which other laws—the precepts—are derived. Each principle, in turn, is grounded in a *person*—in the very character of God himself.
>
> To illustrate, here is a precept from the book of Exodus: "If someone steals an ox or sheep and then kills or sells it,

the thief must pay back five oxen for each ox stolen, and four sheep for each sheep stolen" (22:1). This precept is a specific instance that forbids stealing animals from another person. This precept related to the stealing of animals is grounded in a broader, more inclusive principle of honesty that forbids stealing of any kind, lying, deceit, fraud, and the like. The principle of honesty, however, finds its genesis in the very character of God who is true and right. "He is a faithful God who does no wrong; how just and upright he is" (Deuteronomy 32:4). The precepts give us the commands, and the principles give us the "why" behind the commands. But every biblical precept that leads to a broader principle directs us back to the person of God.

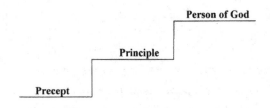

We know that morals are universal when they are grounded in the very nature of God who is absolutely "righteous in everything he does" (Psalm 145:17), "the one who is holy and true" (Revelation 3:7), "there is no evil in him" (Psalm 92:15). But God is not behind the principles and precepts simply to validate the rules; he is there as a person for the purpose of relationship.

The Bible says that God spoke to Moses "face to face, as one speaks to a friend" (Exodus 33:11). Afterward Moses prayed, "If you are pleased with me, teach me your ways so I may know you" (Exodus 33:13 NIV). Moses recognized that learning God's ways—understanding his precepts and the principles behind them—would acquaint him with the person of God himself. Ultimately God doesn't simply want our strict obedience to a set of rules and commands. As he told Hosea the prophet, "I want you to show love, not offer sacrifices. I want you to know me more than I want burnt offerings" (Hosea 6:6). This is why Jesus said, "And this is the way to have eternal life—to know you, the only true God, and Jesus Christ, the one you sent to earth" (John 17:3). God wants to be in relationship with his creation.

But practically everything we know about God comes from the Bible. And most people today see the Bible as merely a religious book for the Christian faith. Your children probably hold that view, too. So what do you say to those who claim the following:

> *Your ideas of morality are rooted in your religious belief from a two- to three-thousand-year-old book. That's fine, but your views of what is right or wrong morally can't trump what Muslims or Hindus or Buddhists or any other religious book teaches. If you say your religious views are right and everyone else's are wrong, you're a religious bigot!*

How do you respond to this?

_____

_____

_____

_____

_____

How would you describe the Bible? It contains moral teachings and is full of laws and instruction for how to live. But what is the Bible actually? Read 2 Timothy 3:16.

Have someone in the group read the following paragraphs aloud, which are drawn from chapter 4 of *The Beauty of Intolerance*.

When you discuss the Bible with family and friends, do not refer to it simply as a spiritual book that teaches us how to live, but as a road map leading one toward the discovery of true reality. The biblical narrative about moral truth teaches that the Creator God revealed himself to Moses and the prophets at given points in history. While the Bible contains poetry, psalms, apocalyptic literature, and parables, it is ultimately a true account of God's relationship with humanity. Moses and the other writers of scripture documented their encounters and messages from God, and these encounters are substantiated by historical evidences.

Yes, scripture is the source of Judaism and Christianity, which are religions. Yet the Bible is unique among all other religious writings in that it is based on historical events backed up by credible historical evidence. The Creator of the world revealed himself first to Moses and the prophets saying, "I am the LORD; there is no other God. I have equipped you. . .so that all the world from east to west will know there is no other God. I am the LORD, and there is no other" (Isaiah 45:5–6). He then took on flesh and revealed himself in the person of Jesus, God's Son. The New Testament writer said, "Long ago God spoke many times and in many ways to our ancestors through the prophets. And now in these final days, he has spoken to us through his Son. God promised everything to the Son as an inheritance, and through the Son he created the universe" (Hebrews 1:1–2).

If the Bible can be proven to be historically inaccurate; if Christ's claim to be God is not historically credible; and if Christ's resurrection can be shown to be a hoax, then Christianity is not a religion worth trusting in. By this view there are certainly good moral teachings in the Bible on how to live and treat one another. But without assurance of the authenticity of Christ's deity, death, and resurrection, they are nothing more. If the Bible were no more than that, it could offer no hope of a life after death. The apostle Paul concluded that if Christ wasn't who he claimed to be and did not bodily rise from the dead, "we are more to be pitied than anyone in the world" (1 Corinthians 15:19).

But of course that is not the case. Considerable evidence exists to prove that the God-breathed words of scripture are historically reliable. And when you share those evidences with your children, they inevitably come face-to-face with the claims of Christ. At that point, if they're honest with themselves, they will encounter an inescapable conclusion: scripture accurately reveals that Jesus is the risen Christ and the only way to the one true God. Of course, that conclusion flies in the face of their cultural conditioning. But with repeated emphasis on how the Bible is historically accurate and reliable, you will likely be able to equip your children to see God's Word for what it is—a true revelation of the one true God and his Son Jesus as the Savior of the world.

Have you ever had a person question the Bible's authority or reliability—that it is not an accurate revelation from God? Are you aware that people do question the historical reliability of scripture? How have you responded or how would you respond to such criticism of God's Word? Share your story.

_____

_____

_____

## APPLYING IT THIS WEEK

This week, share with a friend or a family member why moral truth from God's Word is universally true. Here are some conversation starters to help you:

1. Many people believe morality is situational, individually determined, and not universally true for everyone. Do you believe that? Why or why not?

_____

_____

_____

_____

_____

2. I have been studying what makes moral truth universal. I've been learning. . .

_____

_____

_____

3. In a devotional time between you and God, read Psalm 119:33–40. Make this your prayer. Write a heartfelt prayer of thanks that God has given you his Word to know him and his ways.

_____

_____

_____

_____

_____

This week, before the next group meeting, read chapters 3 and 4 in *The Beauty of Intolerance*. These chapters will solidify and expand on what you have learned in this session.

## CLOSE IN PRAYER

Pray that the truth you have encountered will become more real, alive, and active in your life. Use this prayer time to express your desire to more effectively share with others how God is your source of strength, the one who teaches you right from wrong and how to love and accept others as he does.

SESSION 3

---

# DOES LOVE
# MAKE IT RIGHT?

# WHAT DO YOU THINK?

Over the years, we have interacted with thousands of parents, youth workers, pastors, and Christian educators about what concerns them most about the future of their youth. When you love people, you want to see them protected from those things that would cause them pain and heartache. Venture a guess as to the top two or three concerns that surface as a major concern on the part of Christian families and the church. (Concerns like the use of illegal drugs, alcohol abuse, violence, the loss of Christian faith, premarital sex, lying/cheating, forming unhealthy relationships, etc.)

I think the top concerns would include (identify two or three):

_____

_____

_____

Christian families and church leaders have consistently identified their top concerns as young people walking away from the church and the Christian faith, forming unhealthy relationships, and engaging in premarital sex.

Why do you think most Christian parents and church leaders want young people to refrain from premarital sex? To bring it closer to home, why do you want your children to resist sexual pressure?

_____

_____

_____

_____

_____

_____

# SESSION OBJECTIVE

**To determine what love is and how it leads a person to engage in sexual relations when it is right according to God and his Word.**

## HOW DO YOU RESPOND?

In our ongoing story of Renee and her parents, she inferred that because she and Tony loved each other, it justified their sleeping together. If Renee's parents truly loved their daughter, wouldn't they want what she wanted? Wouldn't they avoid trying to force their standards of morality on their daughter and simply celebrate their daughter's love for her boyfriend?

_____

_____

_____

Statement: *Validating someone else's behavior or belief is the loving thing to do.* Do you agree or disagree with this statement? Why or why not?

_____

_____

_____

_____

Have someone read aloud 1 Corinthians 13:4–5. Based on these verses, what does love do?

_____

_____

_____

First Corinthians 13 describes some things that love does and doesn't do. But if you were to describe the nature of real love, what is love really all about? What is real love motivated by?

_____

_____

_____

Have someone in the group read the following paragraphs aloud, which were adapted from chapter 5 of *The Beauty of Intolerance*.

Cultural tolerance has distorted the idea of relationships and love. It advocates the equality of all moral truth and asserts that no one has the right to hold up a standard of morality for all. And in the process, cultural tolerance twists and distorts the true essence of what love is.

Real love isn't an unlimited endorsement of just any behavior a person chooses to engage in. Many of those behaviors are inherently and inevitably harmful, and to endorse, approve, and encourage them in that behavior is not loving; it is cold and uncaring. If we care about another person, we won't approve behavior that is damaging and destructive to that person's life. On the other hand, expressing real love doesn't involve condemning people when we find their behavior objectionable and contrary to scripture. Real love, biblical, Godlike love, exposes cultural tolerance as the counterfeit of love because it fails to point people to a universal standard of morality designed to save them from serious harm. Cultural tolerance does not address what is in the best interest of a person—it possesses no moral standard that aligns to what is universally right and good. Real love, on the other hand, looks out for the best interest of others, and sometimes that kind of love will mean addressing destructive choices and behaviors in the people we love.

Truth is our best friend, and it is an inseparable part of what real love is. While cultural tolerance may disguise itself as caring, understanding, and loving, it lacks the moral authority of an authentic love that looks out for the best interest of others. A fundamental quality of authentic, real love—it is always other-focused.

Real love is other-focused. Kenton, the father of Renee, was finding it difficult to be other-focused when he discovered his daughter was sleeping with her boyfriend. What are some things that hindered Kenton from being other-focused when confronted with his daughter's behavior? What hinders you from being other-focused when your child engages in acts you have taught him or her not to engage in?

_____

_____

_____

_____

_____

_____

Have someone read aloud Matthew 7:12; Matthew 22:39; Ephesians 5:28–29; and Philippians 2:4.

As we can see by these scripture verses, true love is other-focused. But the question remains, how do we exercise true love while at the same time disagreeing with a person's wrong choices about morality? How do we blend real love with traditional tolerance that looks beyond the faults and failures of others and accepts them for who they are? How do you define that kind of love? Try your hand at defining what God's kind of love is.

Real love is making

_____

_____

_____

Have someone read aloud the following:

> Whatever definition you wrote out, it no doubt included the idea of valuing the interest of the other person as important as your own. Here is another possible way to express that in writing:
>
> *Real love is making the security, happiness, and welfare of another person as important as your own.*
>
> This kind of love, authentic love, protects the loved one from harm and provides for his or her good. When two people exercise this kind of love in a relationship, each looks to provide for the other's best and protect the other from the worst. Because its priority is seeking the best interest of the loved one, real love will not do things that are harmful to the security, happiness, and welfare of another person.
>
> Why is Kenton upset that his daughter is sleeping with her boyfriend? Is it merely because it violates the moral values he tried to teach his daughter? Is it because it may somehow embarrass him or reflect badly on his standing with his Christian friends or the church? That should not be Kenton's primary concern. His primary concern should be his daughter's best interest. When he makes the security, happiness, and welfare of his daughter as important to him as his own, it focuses his attention on how Renee's improper

behavior can negatively affect her physically, spiritually, emotionally, and relationally.

What if Renee and Tony, and our young people today, expressed a providing and protecting kind of love toward one another? Would that kind of love make a sexual relationship right? If so, how?

_____

_____

_____

_____

_____

_____

Have someone read aloud the following:

When true love is founded on the biblical standard of sex, it wants to have sexual relations within the context it was meant to be expressed in—marriage. If Tony truly loved Renee and Renee truly loved Tony, they would wait to engage in sex until they committed to each other in marriage.

When two lovers marry, they are making a public vow committing to provide for and protect each other through thick or thin. That kind of committed love compels a couple to wait to engage in sex until after marriage—which is the context in which love makes it right.

Endorsing immoral behavior is not equivalent to loving a person. Real love speaks the truth because living within the boundaries of God's moral truth is in every person's best interest.

Let's examine how living within God's boundaries is in a person's best interest in regard to sexual morality and why ultimately sexual immorality is wrong.

Have someone read aloud 1 Corinthians 6:18; Ephesians 5:3; and 1 Thessalonians 4:3.

Accepting that God designed sexual relations to be exclusively between a man expressing his love to a woman and a woman expressing her love to a man, then what kind of sexual expression would be considered sexually immoral?

_____

_____

_____

By respecting scriptural boundaries of sexual morality and prohibitions for extramarital and premarital sex, what kind of protection and provision might one expect? List as many as you can by asking, "What are we protected from and what are we provided for when we live sexually moral lives?" One example is offered.

| Protection from... | Provision for... |
|---|---|
| Guilt | Spiritual Rewards |
|  |  |
|  |  |
|  |  |
|  |  |
|  |  |
|  |  |
|  |  |

Share an example from your own life or from someone you know who has reaped the benefits (protection and provision) of abstaining from premarital sex or avoiding extramarital affairs. Be specific as to what protection or provision was experienced.

_____

_____

_____

_____

_____

Have someone read aloud the following:

> Experiencing the "provide and protect" benefits can definitely maximize a person's sex life in marriage. For example, I (Sean) made a clear choice to wait until I made the loving commitment of marriage before experiencing sexual relations. That commitment meant I would remain sexually celibate until I met and married my high school sweetheart (Stephanie) and then remain faithful to her. Stephanie made that same commitment. And because we both were obedient to God's commands regarding sex, we have been protected from feelings of guilt and have enjoyed a consistent relationship with him.
>
> We never had to go through the heartache of a pregnancy before marriage. Consequently, we have not experienced the heart-wrenching ordeal of planning an adoption or struggling with getting married before we were ready.
>
> We have been protected from the fear that any sexually transmitted disease might come into our marriage bed.
>
> We have been protected from the sexual insecurity that can come from being compared to past sexual lovers

one's spouse may have had. And consequently, we have experienced the provision of trust in our relationship.

We have been protected from the emotional distress that premarital sex can bring and the feelings of betrayal that an extramarital affair can cause. As a result, we have enjoyed relational intimacy together unobstructed by breaches of trust or ghosts from the past. And even more than avoidance of these negative consequences, obedience has helped bring an atmosphere of joy, freedom, life, and happiness that God desires each of us to experience. I don't want to portray our relationship in a Pollyannaish manner, as if we don't have any struggles. Like every other couple, of course we do. But this is an area where following God's commandments has benefited us immensely—more than we ever could have imagined when we were younger.

What are the qualities or boundaries that makes sex right? Have someone read aloud 1 Thessalonians 4:3–5, 7 and Hebrews 13:14.

_____

_____

_____

Finish this sentence: The marriage relationship should be kept

_____.

Share an example from your own life or from the life of someone you know that demonstrates how being pure or remaining pure in marriage has an impact emotionally, mentally, relationally, physically, or spiritually.

_____

_____

_____

Have someone read aloud the following.

> To be pure sexually is to "live according to God's original design,"
> without allowing anything to come in to ruin his ideal plan
> for sex. Sex was designed to be experienced between one man
> (husband) and one woman (wife) in a lifelong committed
> marital relationship. To have more than one sexual partner
> would be to bring a foreign substance into the relationship,
> and that relationship would cease to be pure. If you were to
> drop a dirty pebble into a glass of pure water, it would become
> adulterated—impure. A glass of water without any impurities
> in it is an unadulterated glass of water. God wants our sex lives
> to be unadulterated.

Where did the idea of being pure sexually originate? Have someone
read aloud 1 Peter 1:16 and 1 John 3:3.

_____

_____

_____

Finish this sentence: The reason chastity is moral and promiscuity is
immoral is because God is _____.

Have someone read aloud Malachi 2:16 and Mark 10:9.

Finish this sentence: What couples do at a wedding is commit to be
_____ to one another.

What does being faithful say to a spouse's emotions? Perhaps share what a faithful husband or wife means to you emotionally.

_____

_____

_____

_____

_____

_____

Have someone read aloud the following:

> I (Josh) have traveled away from home for most of my married life. I have had more than one opportunity to be unfaithful to Dottie. But in over forty years of marriage, by God's grace I have resisted temptation and demonstrated loyalty, faithfulness, and devoted commitment to only one love-and-sex relationship in my life. And that, of course, is my relationship with Dottie. That commitment means the world to her. It deepens her sense of worth, and it gives her security and tells her she is loved. Of all the billions of women on this planet, she is the one and only lover for me.

Where did the idea of being faithful sexually originate? Someone read Deuteronomy 7:9 and 1 Corinthians 1:9.

_____

_____

_____

Finish this sentence: The reason fidelity in marriage is honorable and infidelity is not is because God is _____.

Have someone read aloud the following:

> Countering the influence that cultural tolerance has had on our young peoples' understanding of sexual morality isn't necessarily easy. We need to take time to intentionally instill God's design for sex. Correcting the distorted view our young people may have about love and sex involves imparting a clear understanding of who God is, who we are in relationship to him, and how he has given us a way of relating to one another and a model for doing it. This biblical narrative about God and his truth is about a way of living and thinking that must be incrementally and consistently imparted to our children. God's instructions for instilling the truth of scripture into young people are as fitting for us today as they were when he first gave them to Israelite parents: "Repeat them again and again to your children. Talk about them when you are at home and when you are on the road, when you are going to bed and when you are getting up" (Deuteronomy 6:7).

## APPLYING IT THIS WEEK

This week, share with a friend or a family member about how real love makes sex right. Here are some conversation starters to help you.

1. I have been studying lately about what some people say makes sex outside of marriage morally okay. Some say love makes it right. What do you think?

_____

_____

_____

2. Our small group has been discussing the concept that love makes sex right. I've been learning. . .

_____

_____

_____

3. In a devotional time before God, read Proverbs 5:3–14. Write out a prayer asking God to help you guide others to follow in God's ways so they can enjoy him and his loving protection and provision.

_____

_____

_____

_____

_____

This week before the next group meeting, read chapter 5 of *The Beauty of Intolerance*. This chapter will solidify and expand on what you have learned in this session.

## CLOSE IN PRAYER

Pray that the truth you have encountered will be more real, alive, and active in your life. Use this prayer time to express your desire to guide the people in your life to follow in God's loving ways so they can enjoy his provision and protection.

# A LOVE THAT ACCEPTS WITHOUT CONDITION

## WHAT DO YOU THINK?

You may expect to feel accepted by those who truly love you. Yet feeling completely accepted by someone who doesn't approve of your behavior is rare. Think of a time in your childhood, or even now, of someone who accepted you without condition, regardless of what you had done. Share your experience.

_____

_____

_____

_____

_____

## SESSION OBJECTIVE

**To learn what it takes to express a love
that accepts another without conditions
regardless of his or her behavior.**

## HOW DO YOU RESPOND?

Someone read aloud 1 Corinthians 6:9–10. A number of sins are highlighted in those verses. For various reasons some Christians have had a more difficult time truly accepting in love while still not approving of those who commit homosexual acts over other acts that are identified in 1 Corinthians. Why do you think some Christians find it difficult to express a loving acceptance toward those who engage in homosexual behavior?

_____

_____

_____

_____

_____

In our previous story Todd, Chad's father, was finding it difficult to convince his son he accepted members of the gay community without approving of them. Let's revisit them hours later as Todd goes to his son's room in an attempt to smooth things over.

Have someone in the group read the following paragraphs aloud, which are adapted from chapter 6 of *The Beauty of Intolerance*.

"Can we talk?" Todd asked as he poked his head into Chad's room.

"I don't want to fight with you, Dad."

"I don't want to fight either. I just want you to know I don't hate your friend's brother or anyone else."

Todd entered the room and sat on the edge of the bed. Chad nodded slightly as he closed his laptop. "I know you don't hate people, Dad. I was just really angry when I said those things."

"I know," Todd responded reassuringly. "But I want you to know I don't hate gay people." Chad looked at his dad but said nothing.

"All I'm trying to say," Todd continued, "is that there are certain things that are wrong, and I'm sorry that you're offended because I believe what I believe."

"But your beliefs are causing you to reject a person for being who he is."

"I'm not rejecting anyone. I'm just standing up for what's right and pointing out what's wrong—and son, whether you agree with it or not, homosexuality is wrong."

"Because you believe that doesn't make it wrong for

everyone," Chad stated firmly. "And when you say the people at the gay games are wrong, you are rejecting them big-time. You are putting them down as human beings and—"

"I'm not putting them down," Todd interrupted.

"You are, too," Chad countered. "Being gay is who Mike's brother is—he didn't choose to be gay; he was just born that way. And you are making him out like he's a pervert or something."

"Well, homosexuality is sinful, son. It's not the way God designed us—it's unnatural."

"Can you hear yourself, Dad?" Chad countered as he shook his head in disapproval. "You have no right to judge like that. You've got to accept people for who they are."

———

Chad and most in our culture today believe the Christian community is being judgmental for condemning the sexual practices of people who claim they were born with a predisposition toward the same sex. Whether homosexuals are born that way or not, how do you think Christians should respond to someone who is gay? How far can loving acceptance of another go before it communicates you approve of his or her behavior? Discuss this together.

_____

_____

_____

_____

_____

_____

Cultural tolerance and its narrative about the truth of who we are as individuals allows no differentiation between who a person is and that person's beliefs, behavior, or lifestyle. If it were written as an equation, it would look like this:

$$\text{Who I Am} = \text{What I Do}$$

Based on this narrative, who you are is inseparable from what you do and think and believe; your identity is wrapped up in your conduct. It stands to reason then, if people express any disagreement with your beliefs, they are disparaging you. If others say your behavior is wrong, they are judging you. When your actions are criticized, you are being criticized. If people can't accept the validity of your lifestyle, then they are being intolerant of you.

Is this concept of personhood correct? Why or why not? Can you think of any scripture passages that offers insight into this issue?

_____

_____

_____

Have someone read aloud Psalm 103:12 and Isaiah 59:2. Based on these two passages, what can we learn about the nature of sin and humans? How does this help solve the misconception that "I am what I do"?

_____

_____

_____

Have someone in the group read the following paragraphs aloud, adapted from chapter 6 of _The Beauty of Intolerance_.

We are not what we do. Our genetic disposition or how we behave does not define who God created us to be. God created humans in his image, which gives them immense dignity and worth (see Genesis 1:26–27).

Although sin has separated us from God, his original intent for us and the reality that we were created in his image have not changed. What we do or don't do may distort that image, but God separates who we are from what we do. That is why he can accept us without condition.

What distinguishes God's unconditional acceptance from that of our culture is authentic love. His love is intended to make the security, happiness, and welfare of another as important as his own. It is other-focused, not performance-focused. God knows the real truth about us—that we were created in his image—and that truth allows him to separate the person from performance. God unconditionally accepts us for who we are without approving of what we do, because he separates the value of the person from the acts of the person.

God can respond with such grace toward us, even in our sin, because he sees a distinction between our "essence" and our "nature." Our essence is that we are beings created in his image with great dignity and worth. Our nature is malignantly infected because of sin. He actually views the condition of sinfulness separate from the essence of who we are as his lost children. The Bible says that "your iniquities have separated you from your God" (Isaiah 59:2 NIV). Isaiah makes a clear separation between us as God's lost children, created in his image, and what we do—sin. It is clear that what we do is not the same as who we are. If that were the case, God couldn't remove "our sins as far away from us as the east is from the west" (Psalm 103:12 TLB). He cannot remove us from our essence, but by his grace through Christ he can transform our nature.

Even though God's holiness cannot embrace our infected life of sin, he freely offers humans salvation because of his love (John 3:16–21). So despite our sinfulness, he offers us grace. And it is that grace—favor that is not merited—that cost him dearly.

In effect God says, "You are my child, created in my image. That is who you are. Your misbehavior is wrong. My holiness cannot overlook that. In fact, I hate what it has done to you—it has separated you from me. So my love compels me to sacrifice my only Son and allow him to endure a cruel death on the cross. This satisfies the requirement of both my holiness and justice. And if you will accept my Son's death as yours, his sacrifice will atone for your sins. I then can forgive you and transfer you from death to life. Because I can see you through the lens of Christ's sacrifice, I can remove the curse of sin from you. Then you will no longer be my lost and dead child, but my found child who will be alive in relationship with me."

God's undeserved love and acceptance through the sacrifice of Christ and imputation of his righteousness to our account are able to remove our sins and restore each of us as individuals created in his image with great dignity and worth. And more than anything, he wants us to be free of a life of wrongdoing so we can know God personally and enjoy him.

What does loving acceptance without condition look like when it comes to those of whom you can't approve? Think of a family member, colleague, or neighbor whose behavior seriously violates a biblical command. What do your actions and attitude sound like and look like when you separate his or her *being* as a person created in God's image from his or her *behavior*?

_____

_____

_____

_____

_____

Share openly, including any struggles you might have, about how separating a person's being from behavior can be difficult and possibly misinterpreted by others.

_____

_____

_____

Have someone read aloud Psalm 103:8–12.

Think of a time when you clearly did wrong, and instead of getting the punishment you deserved, God loved you without condition and forgave you. Did his loving acceptance motivate you to take advantage of his grace and do more wrong, or did it cause you to want to please him even more? Share honestly from your own experience any examples that illustrate this point.

_____

_____

_____

Let's go back to our running stories of Renee and Chad. What positive difference could it make if these parents expressed an authentic, Christlike love and acceptance toward their children?

_____

_____

_____

Have someone in the group read the following paragraphs aloud, adapted from chapter 7 of *The Beauty of Intolerance*. We pick up with Renee's mother (Teri) responding to the idea of having the boyfriend Tony as a house guest.

"That's a wonderful idea, honey," Teri said. "Your dad and I would love it. Just let us know ahead of time which days you'll be here, and I'll have the guest room ready."

Renee hesitated. "Sure Mom. But—" She took a deep breath. "Well, like, is the guest room really necessary? I was thinking we could just stay in my room together."

"Oh," Kenton responded with a sigh. Teri sat silently, trying to keep her face from showing the disappointment she felt inside.

"I know it's a lot to ask and everything," Renee began. "But since Tony and I are rooming together at college anyway, I thought we could room together here, too."

Teri's heart pounded like drums. She looked over at Kenton, his shoulders slumped—his eyes gazing at the floor. Teri spoke first.

"You must really like Tony."

"I do, Mom. In fact, we're in love."

"Love's a great thing," Teri replied. "Your dad and I fell in love while we were in college. But we didn't sleep together before we were married. We weren't perfect, but we avoided a lot of the pain we saw our friends go through because they didn't wait."

"I hear you," Renee responded. "But that's a bit old-fashioned these days."

"It probably does seem old fashioned," Kenton chimed in, speaking softly. "But the emotional, spiritual, and possibly the physical consequences aren't old-fashioned at all."

"I know all about safe sex, Dad," Renee responded quickly.

"It's more than about safe sex, honey. What your mom and I are trying to say is that you mean the world to us and we want what's best for you—so does God. This is from my heart: You'll never regret waiting, but—" Kenton's voice cracked. He paused to regain his composure. "But you may always regret not waiting."

Kenton fought back his emotions. Teri stepped toward her daughter, her eyes blurred with tears, and wrapped her arms around her.

"I love you, honey."

"I love you, too, Mom," Renee whispered. As the two drew apart, a small tear could be seen in the corner of Renee's eye. She took a deep breath.

"I know you guys love me. That means a lot. So about Tony—when he's here we'll sleep in separate rooms. And I promise I will think about what you guys have said."

Kenton stood and took a deep breath.

"Hey," he said, smiling. "How about ol' Dad fixing my pancake special for my college girl?"

"That sounds fantastic, Dad."

———·—·———

Kenton and Teri may not have changed Renee's moral values, and she may still continue sleeping with her boyfriend. But what positives do you envision can come out of parents responding to a college-age child in this way? Discuss together.

_____

_____

_____

Have someone continue to read aloud the situation between Todd and his son Chad. We pick up with Chad explaining he and his friend Mike are headed for a relay race at the locally sponsored Gay Games.

"Ohhhhh, those games. Yeah, I've read some about them. What event are you interested in?"

"My brother's relay race starts in about an hour," Mike said.

*I'm not wild about my son going to these games,* Todd thought. *But maybe there's an opportunity here.*

"Would you guys mind if I join you? I used to run the relay myself."

Chad and Mike looked at each other and shrugged in unison.

"Sure, Dad, come on. There's no entrance fee or anything," Chad stated as he waved his arm toward the door.

As Todd drove the two boys to the games, he learned that Mike's brother had recently told his parents, who were divorced, that he was gay. Todd asked how his parents handled that news. Mike replied that it was not well received. He said his dad told his brother he couldn't stay at his house, and his dad hadn't spoken to his brother since.

After the relay race was over, Todd dropped Mike off at his house. On the drive home, Todd posed a question to his son.

"What do you think about how Mike's dad has responded to his brother being gay?"

"I think it really sucks," Chad stated bluntly.

"Yeah, it's gotta really hurt Mike, too. But why do you think his dad won't even talk to his brother?" Todd probed.

"His dad probably hates gay people, and now that his son's gay, he probably hates him, too."

"You know something, son? You don't have to hate someone just because you disapprove of what he does."

———

Todd went on to share how he and his son could possibly befriend Mike's brother. Chad knew his dad didn't believe homosexual behavior was right. But by Todd being at the relay race, what do you imagine it said to Chad about loving acceptance versus approval? Share any situation you have had in accepting gay people without conveying your approval of their behavior.

_____

_____

_____

_____

_____

_____

_____

_____

_____

_____

_____

_____

# APPLYING IT THIS WEEK

This week share with a friend or a family member how God separates our wrongdoing from who we are created in his image and how he makes a difference between loving acceptance and approval of wrong behavior. Here are some conversation starters to help you.

1. I have been studying lately about the difference between loving acceptance and approval. How do you think a person can make others feel truly accepted and still not approve of their behavior?

_____

_____

_____

2. Our small group has been discussing the idea of accepting others in love without approving of their behavior. I've been learning. . .

_____

_____

_____

3. In a devotional time before God, read Psalm 103:1–18. Write out a prayer asking God to help you extend grace, love, and acceptance to others like he does to you.

_____

_____

_____

This week before the next meeting, read chapters 6 through 8 of *The Beauty of Intolerance*. These chapters will solidify and expand on what you have learned in this session.

## CLOSE IN PRAYER

Use this prayer time to praise God for all the grace, love, and acceptance he has shown toward you and your family.

# CULTURAL TOLERANCE AND YOU

# WHAT DO YOU THINK?

Cultural tolerance is the idea that every person's beliefs, values, lifestyle, and perception of truth claims are equal. This means that moral truth is relative and subjectively determined by the individual.

Have you personally confronted cultural tolerance being played out in today's educational system, government, or society in general? Share an incident where you have observed cultural tolerance being displayed somehow in your interaction with people, in a business, or at an institution.

_____

_____

_____

_____

_____

_____

# SESSION OBJECTIVE

**To address three misconceptions that tend to fuel the idea of cultural tolerance, even within the church.**

# HOW DO YOU RESPOND?

Following are three statements about scripture that are true to an extent, yet they contain an element of error or are only partially true. If we are unable to discern the error in these statements, it is possible that we can unintentionally perpetuate the idea that all truth claims are equal and subjectively created.

See if you can determine the error mixed with truth in these statements. Have someone in the group read the following statements aloud, and then respond to them as a group.

1. *The Bible contains truth designed just for me.*
   This statement is true, yet something about it can lead to a misconception about scripture. What is it about this statement that could be considered error?

_____

_____

_____

Have someone in the group read the following paragraphs aloud.

There is no question that God speaks directly to us through his inspired Word. At times his truth is very specific in its application to us and often comes at a time we need it most. God undoubtedly must have designed it for each of us at just the right moment of our lives. This view is not necessarily an incorrect one. It can have implications, however, that fuel the idea that moral truth is subjective.

Have you ever heard someone say something like, "Here is what this passage means to me" or ask you "What does that scripture verse mean to you?" The importance of the words "means to me" and "mean to you" are sometimes indicative of the influence of cultural tolerance. Rather than looking to the biblical text in order to know *the objective* truth, some Christians are actually looking for *their subjective* meaning of the truth.

This is not to minimize the importance of applying scriptural truth to our lives—it is imperative that we do so. However, it is very important to understand that each book of the Bible conveys a specific truth that is objective and true whether or not we capture its application to our lives. In fact, a biblical application depends on understanding the objective meaning of the text. God wants us to discover the objective meaning of his truth and then experience that truth as our own.

What are some practical ways to keep this misconception that God's truth is only subjective from taking root?

_____

_____

_____

2. *What's true for you isn't necessarily true for me.*

Who is to say one theological viewpoint is more right than another? Some Bible-believing Christians are Calvinists while others are Wesleyan-Armenian. Some Christians claim a prayer covering for women is required; others don't. Some Christians praise God with a worship band, while others say musical instruments in the church should be forbidden. These types of differences have lead many Christians to say, "What's true for you isn't necessarily true for me." There is both truth and error in this statement. What is the truth; what is the error?

_____

_____

_____

_____

_____

_____

Have someone read aloud the following paragraphs.

The idea that "what's true for you isn't necessarily true for me" can lead a person to the conclusion that the moral truths from God's Word are all a matter of opinion. This conclusion reveals confusion between the concepts of *truth* and *belief*.

We are all entitled to our own beliefs, but this doesn't mean each of us has our own truths. Our beliefs describe the way we think the world is. Truth describes the objective state of the world regardless of how we take it to be. Beliefs can be relative, but truth cannot. So when we consider the nature of truth—that it is an objective description of reality—it makes no sense to say that something is true for you and not for me.

For example, imagine you have a frugal son. He places his piggy bank on the table and is about to open it up. You ask him how much he believes is in the bank. He says, "I believe there's more than $20 in there." You counter and say, "*I* believe there is less than $20." Can your varying beliefs about how much the bank contains create two distinct truths? The only way to solve the dispute, of course, is to open the piggy bank and count the money. The instant the money is counted, the truth will be revealed and the false beliefs will be exposed. The truth about the exact dollar amount in the bank exists independently of what you or your son believes about it.

It's the same when it comes to moral truths. God's Word becomes the standard of what is morally true because moral truths stem from God's character, revealed in his Word. These truths declare the way things really are. They are not open to being rewritten as if they were merely personal or subjective viewpoints. What we may believe about moral truths doesn't change the fact they are true. So while moral truths are not up for consideration as personal or subjective, beliefs can be. Personal beliefs strongly held are often called "personal convictions."

In the book of Romans, the apostle Paul addressed the fact that some Jewish followers of Christ were conflicted over what eating restrictions they should follow, what festival days they should observe, and on what day they should celebrate the Sabbath. He told them that "those who don't eat certain foods must not condemn those who do, for God has accepted them" (Romans 14:3). And concerning what day they should worship on, he said, "You should each be fully convinced that whichever day you choose is acceptable" (Romans 14:5).

Paul essentially was calling for the Christians in Rome to be tolerant of one another in the traditional sense of the word; that is, to graciously accept a difference they disagreed with. Some of the Jewish Christians were still holding on to certain requirements of the Old Testament law and Jewish worship. Paul had already written to the Galatian church that the Jewish law (not the moral law) was no longer needed. "The law was our guardian until Christ came," he wrote. "And now that the way of faith has come, we no longer need the [Jewish] law as our guardian" (Galatians 3:24–25). But for some in Rome, it was a struggle to let go of the old customs. Paul was appealing to the stronger, more mature Christians to be tolerant of those who were struggling with these issues.

Paul was making the point that there were issues of belief and preference outside of the universal moral law of God that required a personal decision and were between that person and God. Believers needed to be tolerant of each other regarding these choices.

For example, some people feel very strongly that to honor the Lord's Day they must refrain from buying products on

Sunday. Some people feel it is right to place their children in Christian schools and it would be wrong for them to enroll their children in public school. Many of these people don't condemn those who do otherwise, but they see these as personal convictions or beliefs they must follow. The apostle Paul made this point quite clear when he referred to the now superseded Jewish regulations on what foods were pure or impure. "I know and am convinced," Paul said, "on the authority of the Lord Jesus that no food, in and of itself, is wrong to eat. But if someone believes it is wrong [for them], then for that person it is wrong" (Romans 14:14).

What are some ways you can help others and your family distinguish between moral truth and beliefs?

_____

_____

_____

_____

_____

_____

3. *The Bible is God's Word, but experience determines interpretation.*

The Bible is true and authoritative. And while we shouldn't elevate our own personal experiences over scripture, shouldn't we interpret the Bible with our own experiences in mind? For example, say a person is a Christian and truly loves another person and is willing to remain committed to him or her. Don't these two Christians have a right to marry even if they are the same sex? If they experience a relationship with God and truly love each other, doesn't that make it right? Why or why not?

_____

_____

_____

Have someone read aloud the following paragraphs.

Scripture may admonish us not to rely solely on our own experiences to interpret it, but doesn't it caution us not to ignore it all together? Take Jesus' Sermon on the Mount, for example, where he warned against false prophets:

"Beware of false prophets, who come to you in sheep's clothing but inwardly are ravenous wolves. You will recognize them by their fruits. Are grapes gathered from thornbushes, or figs from thistles? So, every healthy tree bears good fruit, but the diseased tree bears bad fruit. A healthy tree cannot bear bad fruit, nor can a diseased tree bear good fruit. Every tree that does not bear good fruit is cut down and thrown into the fire. Thus you will recognize them by their fruits" (Matthew 7:15–20 ESV).

According to some people, Jesus provides a simple test for a genuine prophet: "If something bears bad fruit, it cannot be a good tree. And if something bears good fruit, it cannot be a bad tree." Since some believe traditional Christian teaching on homosexual behavior brings harm to gay people (depression and suicide, for instance), then it must not be biblical. By contrast, embracing monogamous same-sex relationships brings "good fruit" to gay people, and so it must be right.

Some point out this is a question of interpretation, not biblical authority. But the real question is a matter of what the text *means*. Earlier we stated how important it is to consider context. If you read the larger context for this passage, it becomes clear that "bad fruit" is not stressed out people who feel marginalized from society. Rather, according to Jesus' words in context, bad fruit is "everyone who hears these words of mine and does not do them" (verse 26 ESV). And "good fruit" is "everyone then who hears these words of mine and does them" (verse 24 ESV). In other words, *good fruit is characterized by obedience to Christ and to God's commands.* And therefore bad fruit is sin.

The reality is that there are many issues of orthodox teaching that can cause considerable hardship in people's lives. Can you imagine the amount of distress and anger that would be caused if people followed the biblical guidelines on marriage and divorce (Matthew 19:3–12; 1 Corinthians 7)? Millions of Christians would experience angst, stress, depression, and frustration over what they believe are unreasonable demands to remain married to someone with whom they've fallen out of love. Sure, many people choose not to follow this teaching. But do we have the authority to change biblical teaching because it is difficult to live? It is hard to imagine Jesus and Paul adopting such an approach. In fact, based on this experience interpretation, the preaching of the apostles, which lead them to be threatened, beaten, thrown in prison, and even killed, would be considered "bad fruit." And so would Paul's "thorn in the flesh." Even though Paul pleaded with Christ to remove it, he was told, "My grace is sufficient for you, for my power is made perfect in weakness" (2 Corinthians 12:9 ESV). For the sake of Christ, Paul willingly embraced "weaknesses, insults, hardships, persecutions, and calamities" (verse 10 ESV). Should we expect any less?

What are some practical ways to counter this "experience interpretation" within your church, small group, and families?

_____

_____

_____

_____

_____

To apply the message of *The Beauty of Intolerance* to our lives and that of our families, discuss the following practical steps together.

## 1. Develop Deepened Community

Have someone read aloud the following:

> Building coalitions and connecting with other concerned parents and Christian leaders and educators is a good thing. Yet it will not replace the spiritual and relational nature and strength derived from fellowship with an entire body of believers.
>
> Jesus said, "Love each other. Just as I have loved you, you should love each other. Your love for one another will prove to the world that you are my disciples" (John 13:34–35). Genuine and mature Christian community is powerful and winsome. As our young people and the world around us hear and see us lovingly share our lives with one another, they will want what we have.

What are ways you and your group can reflect a deepened community and be a shining example to your families and the outside world?

_____

_____

_____

_____

_____

_____

## 2. Speak the Truth in Love.

Have someone read aloud the following:

> The underlying theme we have repeatedly emphasized throughout these pages is that moral truths come from the loving heart of a God who is motivated to provide for us and to protect us. Moral truth was never meant to be spoken or understood outside of a loving relationship. Being like Christ and speaking the truth in love are synonymous.
>
> We must consistently speak the truth in love until it becomes a way of life. Doing so will equip us emotionally and relationally to help our young people counter cultural tolerance. Our young people need to see us as models of what moral truth looks like within relationship.

None of us can be perfect models of what moral truth looks like. How do we overcome that reality? How can our imperfections work in our favor?

_____

_____

_____

## 3. Build Relationships with People of a Different Mind-Set.

Have someone read aloud the following:

> How can we Christians change the perception that we
> are hateful, bigoted, and intolerant? There is one vital step
> each one of us can take—build genuine relationships with
> people who see the world very differently than we do. We
> will overcome the cultural perception that Christians are
> intolerant bigots only when people hear this claim and their
> first thought is, *That doesn't seem right. I know Christians,*
> *and they're loving, gracious, and thoughtful.* Each one of us
> has a responsibility to build real relationships with people
> who reject our most cherished beliefs. It is easy to build
> relationships with people who are like us. The challenge is to
> build relationships with people who are *un*like us.

What challenges or pitfalls do you see in building relationships with
those who are unlike you, for example, nonbelievers, gays, atheists,
etc.?

_____

_____

_____

_____

_____

_____

_____

_____

What are some ways to go about forming relationships with such people? What would that look like?

_____

_____

_____

_____

_____

## APPLYING IT THIS WEEK

This week share with a friend or a family member how the Bible is God's objective revelation of himself and his truth to all of humanity. Here are some conversation starters to help you.

1. I have been studying lately about some misconceptions about the Bible. Do you think there is truth that is true for you but not necessarily true for other people? Why or why not?

_____

_____

_____

2. Our small group has been discussing common misconceptions about the Bible. I've been learning. . .

_____

_____

_____

3. In a devotional time before God, read Proverbs 2:1–15. Write out a prayer thanking God for the wisdom of his truth and how his Word has guided you and your family in the right path.

This week, read chapters 9 through 12 of *The Beauty of Intolerance*. It will help solidify the message of this fifth session.

## CLOSE IN PRAYER

Use this prayer time to thank God that he has been so faithful to preserve an accurate and reliable revelation of himself and his truth to you and your family.

# GROUP LEADER'S GUIDE

# PURPOSE OF THIS STUDY

Using *The Beauty of Intolerance Study Guide* with a small group means you will have approximately five hours of interaction with them. This study is designed for a one-hour period per session. It is based on *The Beauty of Intolerance* by Josh and Sean McDowell. Drawing directly from the book, it encourages group participants to read certain chapters between sessions. This study, along with the companion book, provides clarity on today's cultural views of tolerance, detects its inaccuracies, and offers practical answers on how to counter its influence on individuals and their families. Upon completing the study, group participants will be better equipped to lead their families to understand how to accept others without necessarily approving of their behavior by expressing God's meaning of real love.

# HOW TO USE THE STUDY GUIDE

The *Beauty of Intolerance Study Guide* is designed to be used interactively by a group and by individuals as well. An individual can certainly benefit by going through it alone; however, more can be experienced and accomplished in a group context.

Each group participant needs a copy of the study guide. (The study guide is not intended to be shared by couples.) Order enough copies so each person attending your group can have one. They can be obtained through your local Christian supplier or by ordering from the publisher at 1-800-852-8010 or www.barbourbooks.com. It is wise to order a few extra copies to cover individuals who may show up at later sessions. Your church may decide to provide the study guides, or you may want to ask each participant to pay something toward the purchase of their resources.

As stated earlier, *The Beauty of Intolerance* book is the companion to the study experience. You will want to encourage participants to read a selection of chapters between sessions. Therefore, consider adding this resource to your order of study guides. Couples can share in the reading of the book, so one book per couple is recommended. You may order the book from your local Christian supplier or by contacting Barbour Publishing as noted above.

# EACH SESSION OF THIS GUIDE IS DIVIDED INTO FIVE AREAS:

## • WHAT DO YOU THINK?

Usually, each session asks someone in your group to read selected paragraphs drawn from *The Beauty of Intolerance*. This is followed by questions posed to your group for interactive discussion. Notes are to be taken and written down in the spaces provided in the study guide.

## • SESSION OBJECTIVE

This simply identifies the outcome you are focused on or the desired objective for your group session.

## • HOW DO YOU RESPOND?

This section of the study guide allows you to prompt your group on how they answer the questions posed. The answers will come from their own knowledge or from an understanding of various scripture passage readings prompted in each session.

## • APPLYING IT THIS WEEK

Here you encourage your group to share what they are
learning with a friend or family member during the week.
A devotional scripture and a prayer time activity are also
provided. You will want to encourage participants to read
the chapter assignments from *The Beauty of Intolerance* as
well. The particular chapters to read are referenced at the
end of the "Apply It This Week" section.

## • CLOSE IN PRAYER

While closing in prayer may seem like the expected thing
to do, we encourage you to make praying together a very
intentional exercise. Pray as a group that the truth you have
encountered will become real, alive, and active in your lives
throughout the week. Use your prayer time to express your
desire to more deeply experience the power and relevance
of God's Word. Praying together is an important part of
making your group experience come alive in each person's
heart and life.

# SUGGESTIONS TO GUIDE
# YOUR DISCUSSION

Interacting with your group about how to respond to cultural tolerance is good, but healthy discussions are those that lead people to more consistently apply God's design to love and accept others as he does. Following are some suggestions in guiding your group discussion to that end.

1. *Don't be afraid of silence.* Some group leaders make the mistake of asking a thought-provoking question and then, when no one answers immediately, moving on too quickly to the next question. The wise leader will try to create an atmosphere in which careful thought is encouraged—by the wise use of silence. Allow a brief time for thought after each question if necessary, then signal for someone to speak up by simply asking, "Anybody?" or "Someone finish your thought out loud."

2. *Let discussion follow its own path without letting the group stray too far.* Don't be in a hurry to move to the next question in the study guide if the discussion is moving forward. But be careful not to let your participants get off on tangents not related to the topic of discussion.

3. *As often as possible, follow a comment with another question.* After a person has made an observation, ask, "Can you think of an example?" or ask the rest of the group for a response.

4. *Don't feel obligated to ask all (or exclusively) the questions in the study guide.* If your group's time is limited, highlight the questions you wish to ask. Add questions suited to your own group as discussion develops.

5. *When it's practical, "prime the pump" of discussion by planting questions with the most vocal, well-spoken participants.* If your group is slow to start discussions, jot one or two questions onto index cards, and give them to some of your most vocal group members before the session, asking them to be ready to offer comments if others don't jump in quickly. You may also ask several confident individuals if they will allow you to call them by name to answer a question if the discussion begins to lag.

6. *Seek attitudinal and behavioral responses.* Don't seek "right" answers as much as truthful discussion. Don't just probe what your group thinks about a topic but how they respond to a question attitudinally or behaviorally. The idea is to search out where each person is on his or her spiritual journey. This isn't to say that wrong attitudes or actions should be agreed with or condoned; it simply means you are creating an atmosphere of transparency and safety where people can open up and be honest with God and their spiritual family.

7. *Finally, refer frequently to scripture as your baseline.* You will notice scripture passages are referred to in this study guide. While opinions may vary on a lot of issues, encourage your group to answer the question, "What does God say on this issue?" And if your participants are to discover what God's position is, his Word is where they must turn. Scripture is your baseline for revealing his truth.

Your role as a group leader or facilitator is significant. May God use your gifts to his glory as you encourage your group to allow God's Word to come alive in their lives.